THE ANCIENT
Mediterranean

THE ANCIENT Mediterranean

REBECCA STEFOFF

BENCHMARK BOOKS

MARSHALL CAVENDISH

NEW YORK

AUTHOR'S NOTE ON DATES

This book spans more than a thousand years of history. The first part of this span falls within the time period now called B.C.E. (for Before the Common Era). B.C.E. dates are numbered backward from the year 1, which marks the beginning of the Common Era (C.E.) a little more than two thousand years ago. When dealing with B.C.E. dates, remember that higher numbers are further away in time than lower ones. To find out how long ago an ancient event occurred, add the current year to the B.C.E. date of the event. For example, if you are reading this book in the year 2010, and you learn that Julius Caesar was assassinated in 44 B.C.E., add 2010 and 44 to find that he died 2,054 years ago.

Benchmark Books · Marshall Cavendish Corporation · 99 White Plains Road · Tarrytown, New York 10591-9001
www.marshallcavendish.com · Copyright © 2005 Rebecca Stefoff · All rights reserved. No part of this book may be reproduced or utilized in any form or by any means electronic or mechanical including photocopying, recording, or by any information storage and retrieval system, without permission from the copyright holders. All Internet sites were available and accurate when sent to press.
Library of Congress Cataloging-in-Publication Data · Stefoff, Rebecca, 1951– · The ancient Mediterranean world / by Rebecca Stefoff.
p. cm. — (World historical atlases) · Summary: Text plus historical and contemporary maps provide a look at the history of cultures that flourished along the Mediterranean Sea. · Includes bibliographical references and index. · ISBN 0-7614-1641-2
1. Mediterranean Region—History—To 476—Juvenile literature. [1. Mediterranean Region—History—To 476.] I. Title
II. Series: Stefoff, Rebecca, 1951– World historical atlases. · DE86.S84 2005 · 938—dc22 · 2003012027
Printed in China · 1 3 5 6 4 2 · Book designer: Sonia Chaghatzbanian

Art and photo research by Linda Sykes Picture Research, Inc., Hilton Head, SC

The photographs in this book are used by permission and through the courtesy of: Noboru Komine/Lonely Planet Images: front cover; Mimo Jodice/Corbis: ii; Roger Wood/Corbis: 6; Gianni Dagli Orti/Corbis: 9, 10; Archivo Iconografica, S. A./ Corbis: 11, back cover; British Museum: 12; Bodleian Library, Oxford, U.K.: 13; Kevin Fleming/Corbis: 14; British Museum/Dagli Orti/The Art Archive: 16; Royalty Free/Corbis: 18; Michael Nicholson/Corbis: 20; Chiaramonti Museum, Vatican/Dagli Orti/The Art Archive: 22; Dave Bartruff/Corbis: 24; Archaeological Museum Naples/Dagli Orti/The Art Archive: 26; The Stapleton Collection/Bridgeman Art Library: 28, 35; Martin Moos/ Lonely Planet Images: 30; Dagli Orti/The Art Archive: 32; Museo di Villa Giulia, Rome/The Art Archive: 33; Museo Capitolino, Rome/Dagli Orti/The Art Archive: 34; Archaeological Museum, Naples/Dagli Orti/The Art Archive: 37; Museé de la Poste, Paris, France/Archives Charmet/Bridgeman Art Library International: 39; Basilica San Vitale Ravenna, Italy/Dagli Orti/The Art Archive: 43.

Contents

CHAPTER ONE

Greece

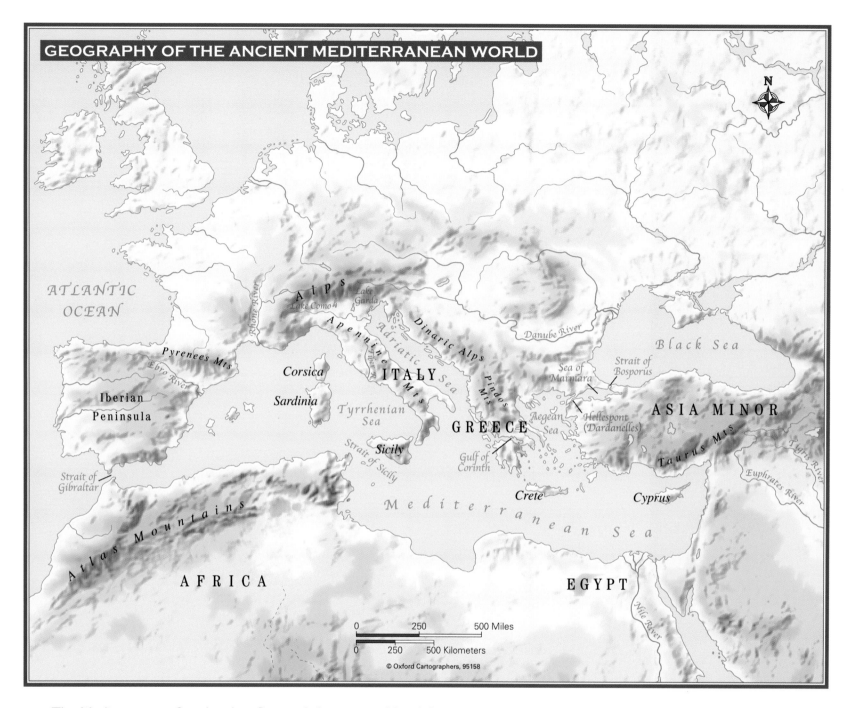

GEOGRAPHY OF THE ANCIENT MEDITERRANEAN WORLD

N

ATLANTIC
OCEAN

Alps

Lake Como
Lake Garda

Rhone River

Apennine Mts

Adriatic

Dinaric Alps

Danube River

Black Sea

Pyrenees Mts

Ebro River

Corsica

ITALY

Tiber

Pindos Mts

Sea of Marmara

Strait of Bosporus

ASIA MINOR

Iberian
Peninsula

Sardinia

Tyrrhenian
Sea

Aegean
Sea

Hellespont
(Dardanelles)

Taurus Mts

GREECE

Tigris River

Strait of Sicily

Sicily

Gulf of
Corinth

Strait of
Gibraltar

Crete

Cyprus

Euphrates River

M e d i t e r r a n e a n   S e a

Atlas Mountains

AFRICA

EGYPT

Nile River

0   250   500 Miles

0   250   500 Kilometers

© Oxford Cartographers, 95158

The Mediterranean Sea deeply influenced the ancient life of the region. It was a source of food, and it also affected the weather, keeping temperatures milder along the coasts than farther inland. Finally, the sea linked the various societies that sprang up along its shores. Once people had learned to build and navigate ships, the Mediterranean Sea became a highway for migration, trade, and conquest.

Several thousand years ago, on a rugged tongue of land jutting into the eastern Mediterranean Sea, a civilization arose that shaped history long after its own collapse. Ancient Greece gave the world its first experiments in democracy, the beginnings of science, and artistic masterpieces that we still admire today. Yet the story of ancient Greece includes darkness and violence as well as greatness. In the end the civilization that laid the foundations for Western culture was overcome by a more powerful empire. But another reason for the fall of the Greeks was that endless fighting among themselves had divided and weakened them.

BRONZE AGE ANCESTORS

Some historians divide **prehistory** into periods based on toolmaking techniques. Using this timetable, Greek history begins in the Bronze Age. After the age of stone tools, but before people learned to forge iron, the best tools and weapons were made of bronze—a blend of copper and tin. In the part of the eastern Mediterranean known as the Aegean Sea, the Bronze Age lasted from about 3000 to 1200 B.C.E. Three cultures that developed during this time were ancestors of Greek civilization.

One culture blossomed between 2500 and 1900 B.C.E. in the Cyclades, islands southeast of Greece. The Cycladic people were farmers who lived in small communities, worshiped **fertility** goddesses, and

Archaeologists have found several small statues of female figures in the remains of ancient settlements on the Cyclades. The discoveries have led experts to believe that the Cycladic people worshiped fertility goddesses, symbols of growth and new life.

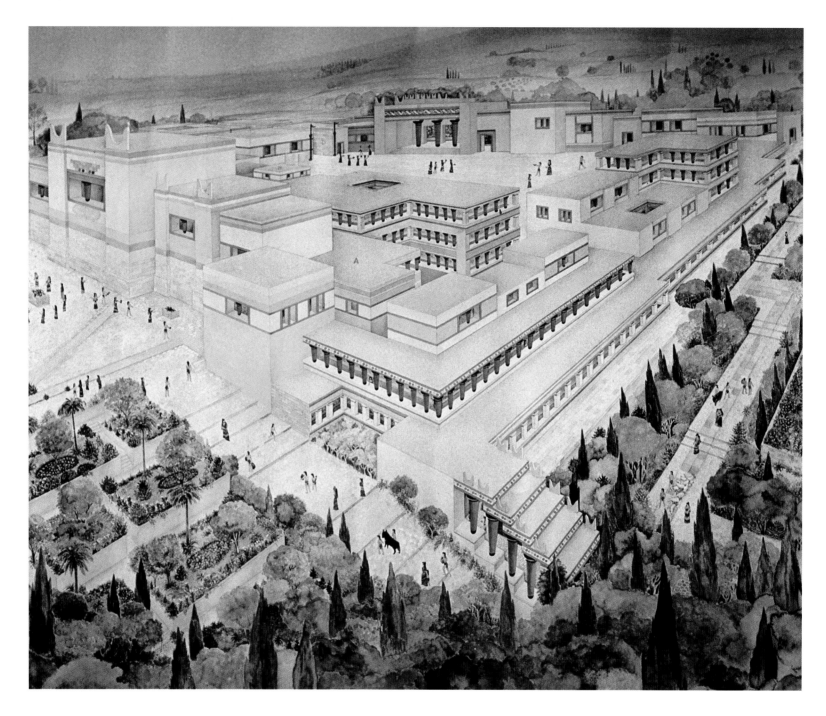

At its peak around 1900 B.C.E., the Minoan palace at Knossos covered 6 acres (2.4 hectares) and housed up to 80,000 people. It had storerooms, workrooms, marketplaces, large open squares, rooms for religious rituals, and royal chambers. A system of stone channels provided fresh water to some of the rooms and carried away waste.

traded with people on the Greek mainland. They left behind a wealth of artwork and **artifacts** made of bronze, marble, silver, and lead, but no written records.

By 2200 B.C.E. a second advanced civilization had risen in the Aegean. It centered on Crete, a large island south of Greece. **Archaeologists** call it Minoan, after King Minos, a character in legends about the island. The Minoans built vast, sprawling structures called palace-complexes, which housed large groups of people and were something like towns, made up of hundreds of rooms under a single roof. The Minoans were skilled seamen who traded with Egypt, mainland Greece, and other islands. But Minoan civilization collapsed around 1400 B.C.E., and Crete came under the control of the Aegean's third Bronze Age culture, the Mycenaeans.

The Mycenaeans rose to power after 2000 B.C.E. in the Peloponnese, the southern part of mainland Greece. They are named for Mycenae, one of their walled fortress cities. Led by warrior kings, the Mycenaeans gained territory and power between 1600 and 1200 B.C.E., shifting the center of Aegean culture from the islands to the Greek mainland. Then, around 1200 B.C.E., two destructive forces began tearing at Mycenaean civilization.

One was a series of invasions of southern Greece by people from the north. The other was warfare among different Mycenaean groups. Forts and palaces burned, farmers abandoned their fields, the skills of reading and writing were lost, and Greece entered a time of war and confusion.

THE DARK AGE

By 1100 B.C.E. the Mycenaean era had ended, and Greece's Dark Age had begun. It was a time of movement and **migration**.

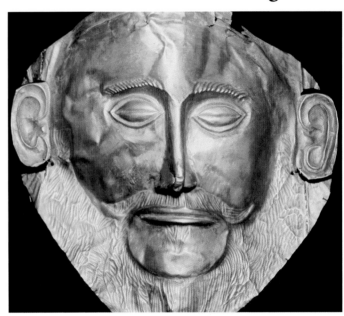

Heinrich Schliemann, the German archaeologist who found this gold mask in a grave at Mycenae in 1876 C.E., said, "I have gazed upon the face of Agamemnon." Schliemann believed that the mask was made for Agamemnon, an ancient king said to have fought in the legendary Trojan War. Modern archaeologists, though, say the mask dates from about 1600 B.C.E., centuries before the Trojan War may or may not have taken place. Yet Schliemann's influence lingers. Many people still call the magnificent funeral ornament the Mask of Agamemnon.

Unsolved Mysteries of the Minoans

Archaeologists have been studying the Minoans since 1900 C.E., when digging began at the ruins of Knossos, one of their largest palaces. Despite more than a century of research, many things about the Minoans remain unknown—especially their language. Two forms of writing were found in the ruins. Scholars call them Linear A and Linear B. Experts decoded Linear B, which turned out to be a form of Mycenaean, or very early Greek. Unfortunately the Linear B writings deal mostly with taxes and lists of stored goods. They contain no clues about the Minoans' history, beliefs, or culture. Such information may exist on the many clay tablets written in Linear A, which may be a non-Greek Minoan language. So far, however, no one has managed to decode Linear A.

Another mystery is the sudden end of Minoan civilization. Did a Mycenaean invasion destroy it? Or did the Mycenaeans simply take over after another force dealt a fatal blow to the Minoans? Ruins on Crete show signs of earthquake and fire damage after 1450 B.C.E., and on the nearby island of Thera a volcano exploded a few years later. These events may have been disastrous for trade and agriculture. By 1380 B.C.E. Crete's palaces had been partly repaired, but by then Mycenaeans controlled them. Archaeologists hope that future finds will shed more light on the fate of the Minoans.

A tablet from Knossos, written in Linear B—an early form of Greek—around 1400 B.C.E. The tablet tells of a gift of olive oil that was presented to the gods.

Again and again, waves of people from the mountainous northern frontier of Greece swept down into the plains and valleys, keeping the region in a state of constant upheaval. The events that had helped destroy Mycenaean civilization would be repeated more than once in the ancient Mediterranean world. Invaders or immigrants from outlying regions would descend upon rich cities and kingdoms, triggering a cycle of war, turmoil, and the breakdown of civilization.

For three centuries Greece was a land of nomads and small villages. Whole stretches of the country were completely empty of inhabitants. Eventually the surviving Mycenaeans settled in scattered groups in Achaea, along the coast of the Gulf of Corinth in the northern Peloponnese. Other new settlements appeared on the Aegean Islands and in Ionia, on the southwestern coast of **Asia Minor** (modern Turkey). Tribes from the north formed permanent settlements as well, occupying the northern coast of the Gulf of Corinth, an area known as Aetolia.

Made in Germany in 1492 C.E., this map of Greece and the Aegean Sea is based on the work of the Greek geographer Ptolemy from thirteen centuries earlier. The map clearly shows Greece's rugged seacoast, its fringe of islands, and the mountain ranges (the brown areas) that divide the country into many isolated regions.

The northerners were not entirely foreign. Their languages were related to Mycenaean, and some of their customs and beliefs resembled those of the inhabitants of Greece. One large and powerful new group, the Dorians, occupied the Peloponnese. As the Dorians and other newcomers mingled with the last of the Mycenaeans, their ways of life blended to create Hellenic, or Greek, culture.

13

A piece of ancient pottery shows a scene from the *Odyssey*, one of several long poems about Greek gods and heroes. The wandering hero Odysseus has tied himself to the mast of his ship so that he can resist the Sirens, mythical figures whose hypnotic songs lured mariners into steering their ships onto the rocks.

GREEK CIVILIZATION IS BORN

The Hellenic culture that emerged from the Dark Age was marked by two opposite qualities. One was unity based on the cultural elements that all Greeks shared: language, religion, and festivals such as the Olympic Games, first held in 776 B.C.E. The other opposing force was political and military conflict among the many Greek regions and states. Disputes and wars would prevent them from ever joining as a single nation.

As Greek civilization took shape, it came into increasing contact with people beyond Greece. After about 800 B.C.E. the Greeks were once again trading with

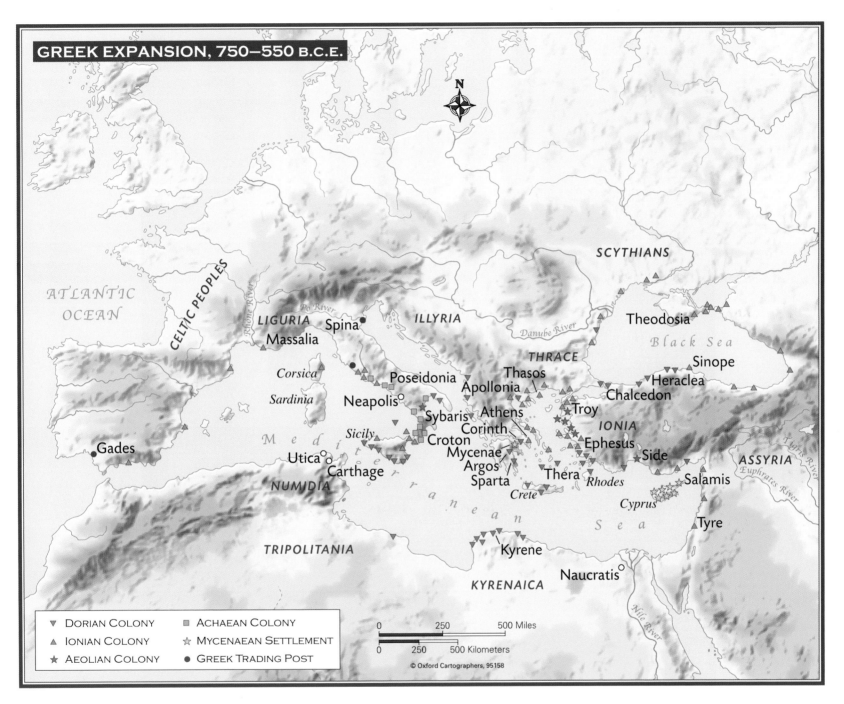

GREEK EXPANSION, 750–550 B.C.E.

ATLANTIC OCEAN

CELTIC PEOPLES

SCYTHIANS

LIGURIA
Massalia
Spina

ILLYRIA

Danube River

Theodosia

Black Sea

Po River

Rhone River

Corsica

Sardinia

Neapolis

Poseidonia

Thasos

Apollonia

THRACE

Sinope

Heraclea

Chalcedon

Sybaris

Athens

Troy

IONIA

Sicily

Croton

Corinth

Ephesus

Gades

Utica

Carthage

Mycenae

Argos

Sparta

Mediterranean

Thera

Rhodes

Side

Crete

Cyprus

Salamis

ASSYRIA

Tigris River

Euphrates River

NUMIDIA

Sea

Tyre

TRIPOLITANIA

Kyrene

Nile River

KYRENAICA

Naucratis

Legend:
- ▼ DORIAN COLONY
- ▲ IONIAN COLONY
- ★ AEOLIAN COLONY
- ■ ACHAEAN COLONY
- ☆ MYCENAEAN SETTLEMENT
- ● GREEK TRADING POST

0   250   500 Miles
0   250   500 Kilometers

© Oxford Cartographers, 95158

The Greek city-states extended their control well beyond their borders. They established dozens of new out-posts beyond the boundaries of their own land. These colonies were called "daughter cities" of the "mother cities" that had founded them. The colonies helped spread Greek language, architecture, and civilization across a wide area. Their influence was especially strong in southern Italy and Ionia (western Turkey), the sites of most of these daughter cities.

This figure of a Persian nobleman decorates a stairway built around 465 B.C.E. in Persepolis, the capital of the Persian empire. The empire conquered many Greek colonies in Ionia and came close to gaining control of parts of the Greek homeland.

other Mediterranean peoples. They learned of an alphabet used by the Phoenicians of the eastern Mediterranean, and they adopted it as the basis of their own written language. With the rebirth of literacy, the Greeks began recording their history and creating their body of literature. Among the first texts written were the *Iliad* and the *Odyssey*, epic poems about a war between Greece and the city of Troy in Asia Minor. These works included **myths** and heroic legends from the Mycenaean age.

By the 700s B.C.E., the Greeks had organized into city-states, political units made up of a central city and the farms, villages, and forests around it. At first, kings ruled many of the city-states. Before long, other forms of government appeared. Some city-states became **republics** in which the citizens chose their leaders. Not all citizens had a voice—generally only rich, noble, or landowning men could vote. Athens eventually adopted the most democratic system, allowing all men except slaves to vote.

Some city-states, such as Sparta, expanded by conquering their neighbors. Others grew by establishing **colonies** outside Greece and Ionia. The colonies produced lumber, minerals, wheat, and other resources for the parent cities, and some colonies became large and wealthy. Through colonization and trade, the Greeks gained a foothold across a wide region, from the Black Sea to the shores of Spain.

THE PERSIAN WARS

While Greek civilization grew and spread, the Persian empire was doing the same, moving beyond its homeland in present-day Iran and gobbling up other states in western Asia. In the late 500s B.C.E. the Persians conquered Asia Minor, including the Greek cities of Ionia. The Ionians rebelled in 499 with the help of Athens, but by 493 the Persians had crushed the revolt in Ionia and decided to attack mainland Greece.

The invading Persians landed at Marathon, near Athens, in 490 B.C.E. In an historic battle 10,000 Greeks overcame the larger Persian force. The defeat, however, only sharpened Persia's determination to conquer its foes. Ten years later the Persian emperor Xerxes led an immense army and navy against Greece. The most powerful Greek city-states, Athens and Sparta, set aside their rivalry to join forces against these invaders. The war ended in 479 after a sea battle in which the Greeks destroyed two hundred Persian ships and lost only forty of their own. Xerxes and the Persians retreated, leaving the Greek city-states to rebuild economies shattered by the high cost of war and to resume struggling among themselves for power.

Perched on a hill called the Acropolis, in the center of Athens, the Parthenon is Greece's most-visited archaeological site and the enduring symbol of Greece's so-called Golden Age. When first built, it was decorated with many brightly painted marble statues and carvings. Their colors have long since faded and flaked away, but the marble forms remain masterpieces of the sculptor's art.

ATHENS AGAINST SPARTA

After the Persian Wars, Athens was determined to become the leader among the Greek city-states. The Athenians formed an **alliance** called the Delian League with the Ionian and Aegean cities, claiming that they should unite their resources in case Persia attacked again. The league's funds enriched Athens, as did the discovery of silver in Athenian territory.

Yet during this time of great success and confidence, Athens was not at peace. The Athenians not only led the Delian League in attacks on Persian ports in Asia Minor, they also seized territory from other Greek city-states. Athens's growing power disturbed its longtime rival, Sparta. In 460 B.C.E. the two city-states went to war, fighting for ten years in the Peloponnese and in Attica, the region around Athens. At the same time Athens found itself again clashing with the Persian empire, this time in Egypt and the Aegean Sea. Some members of the Delian League also rebelled against Athens. By 449, however, Athens had made peace with Sparta, Persia, and the league.

The peace was shortlived. In 431 B.C.E. Athens and Sparta battled again in the Peloponnesian War. Sparta invaded Attica, and Athens swarmed with refugees. **Plague** struck the city, killing more than a third of its people. A turning point in the long war came in 413, when Athens lost many ships and men in a failed attack on a Peloponnesian colony in Sicily. Sparta then joined forces with the Persians, offering the Ionian cities to the Persian empire in return for help against Athens. Sparta was now the greater power, while Athens was severely weakened after almost half a century of war. In 404 the Athenians surrendered.

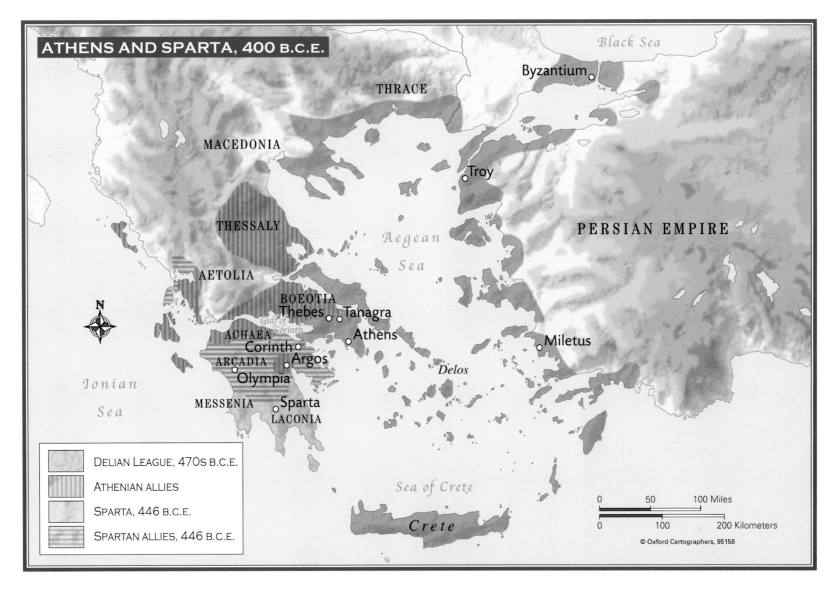

ATHENS AND SPARTA, 400 B.C.E.

Black Sea

Byzantium

THRACE

MACEDONIA

Troy

THESSALY

*Aegean
Sea*

PERSIAN EMPIRE

AETOLIA

BOEOTIA
Thebes Tanagra
Athens

ACHAEA
Corinth
ARCADIA Argos
Olympia

*Ionian
Sea*

MESSENIA Sparta
LACONIA

Miletus

Delos

Sea of Crete

Crete

DELIAN LEAGUE, 470S B.C.E.

ATHENIAN ALLIES

SPARTA, 446 B.C.E.

SPARTAN ALLIES, 446 B.C.E.

0   50   100 Miles

0   100   200 Kilometers

© Oxford Cartographers, 95158

The Peloponnesian War pitted Athens and its allies against Sparta and its own network of supporters. Athens had gained its allies through force and did not treat them as equal partners, so the allies often felt no great loyalty to the city-state. Revolts sprang up, and some former Athenian allies eventually joined forces with Sparta. The Spartan military feared the powerful Athenian navy, so they waged war on land rather than at sea. Year after year, Sparta and its allies marched into Athenian territory, destroying crops and burning homes. But only when Sparta allied itself with the Persian empire did Athens agree to a peace treaty.

Athens remained independent, but Sparta had become the Greek superpower. Testing their strength, the Spartans turned against Persia, fighting to free the Ionian Greeks. To strike a blow against Sparta, Athens now sided with the Persians. Outbreaks of fighting continued between Athens and Sparta until they again had to join forces, this time against the increasingly powerful city-state of Thebes. Soon, though, a new power would change the political picture in Greece and across the ancient Mediterranean world.

CHAPTER TWO

Alexander's Empire

While the Greeks fought among themselves, a small kingdom on their northern border slowly grew in size and strength. One of its kings eventually conquered Greece. Another carried Greek culture and civilization farther than the Greeks themselves had ever reached.

MACEDONIAN MIGHT

The kingdom of Macedonia emerged in the 600s B.C.E. Over the next few hundred years, it was drawn into the struggles of larger powers, first taken over by the Persian empire and then swept up in the rivalry between Athens and Sparta. The kings of Macedonia sided first with Sparta, then with Athens, while trying to keep from being dominated by either.

Despite the difficulty of remaining on peaceful terms with Athens and Sparta, the Macedonian rulers admired Greek culture and thought of their country as part of the Greek world. Macedonia sent athletes to the Olympic Games and princes to be educated in Greek cities. One such prince became King Philip II of Macedonia in 359. Fearing that his kingdom would be swallowed up by the ambitious and aggressive Greek city-states, Philip methodically gained control of one city-state after another

Philip II is remembered today mostly as the father of Alexander the Great, but he was a mighty leader in his own right. Philip more than doubled Macedonian territory and cleverly played the rival Greek city-states against each other. He also planned to invade Persia. But Philip was murdered by an assassin at his daughter's wedding feast before he could carry out the plan. It was Alexander who would go on to invade Persia, changing the history of the ancient world.

through a combination of bribery, alliances, and military strength. By 338 B.C.E. he had conquered all of Greece except Sparta, which had lost much of its power. Philip let the Greeks remain officially independent. However, he set up a council called the League of Corinth to govern them, naming himself the leader of the council.

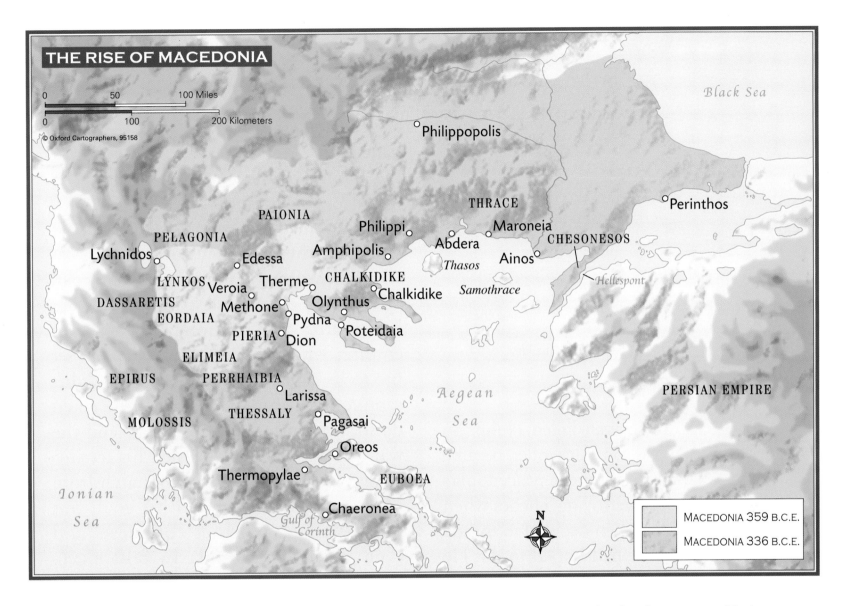

THE RISE OF MACEDONIA

0 50 100 Miles
0 100 200 Kilometers
© Oxford Cartographers, 95158

Black Sea

Philippopolis

THRACE

Perinthos

PAIONIA

PELAGONIA

Philippi

Maroneia

CHESONESOS

Lychnidos

Edessa

Amphipolis

Abdera

Ainos

LYNKOS

Therme

CHALKIDIKE

Thasos

Veroia

Chalkidike

Samothrace

Hellespont

DASSARETIS

Methone

Olynthus

EORDAIA

Pydna

PIERIA

Dion

Poteidaia

ELIMEIA

EPIRUS

PERRHAIBIA

Aegean

PERSIAN EMPIRE

Larissa

Sea

MOLOSSIS

THESSALY

Pagasai

Oreos

Thermopylae

EUBOEA

Ionian

Sea

Chaeronea

Gulf of Corinth

N

MACEDONIA 359 B.C.E.

MACEDONIA 336 B.C.E.

The Peloponnesian War weakened Athens and Sparta but did not bring lasting peace to the Greek city-states. Their continued fighting also drew their attention away from the powers rising outside of Greece. One of these up-and-coming states was Macedonia, whose capital was located at Edessa. Beginning in 359 B.C.E., King Philip II enlarged Macedonian territory. Philip gained control of northern Greece and Thrace, a large region to the east. He did not officially rule Athens, Sparta, or the other southern Greek city-states, but he kept them under close control. His son and heir, Alexander the Great, was of a different mind and considered himself the king of the Greeks as well as the Macedonians.

Darius III of Persia lost several big battles to Alexander, but each time he managed to escape. Alexander declared many times that he would kill Darius, but in the end the Persian king died through betrayal, not battle. To make peace with Alexander, Darius's own officers took his life.

TO RULE THE WORLD

In 336 B.C.E. an assassin killed Philip. So his twenty-year-old son, Alexander, became king. Alexander tightened Macedonia's control of Greece, destroying Thebes when it resisted him. He then decided to invade Persia, as his father had hoped to do. He led a vast army across the Hellespont, a narrow waterway between Europe and Asia Minor, and began a triumphal march of conquest.

Alexander started by defeating local Persian governors and freeing the Greek cities of the Ionian coast. He went on to conquer most of Asia Minor before marching south into Syria, part of the Persian empire. He defeated the army of King Darius III of Persia, destroyed the Persian navy at the port of Tyre, and marched on to Egypt, where he brought an end to Persian rule. The Egyptians hailed him as a hero, a king, and a god. At the mouth of the Nile River, Alexander founded a new capital called Alexandria. It was destined to become one of the great cities of the ancient world, although Alexander soon left and never saw it again.

Determined to crush Darius, Alexander led his army into the heart of the Persian empire, where he captured cities and set fire to its capital, Persepolis. But he didn't capture the Persian king. Before he could do so, Persian officers hoping to end the war killed Darius and turned his territory over to Alexander. The monarch from Macedonia had achieved his goal, but he still sought further conquests and even greater triumphs. In 330 B.C.E. he led his armies east toward the central Asian territory of Bactria (now part of Afghanistan), on the eastern fringe of the Persian empire. After several years and many battles, Alexander conquered the warlike Bactrians, establishing Greek-style military posts along the frontier. He then marched south over the rugged Hindu Kush

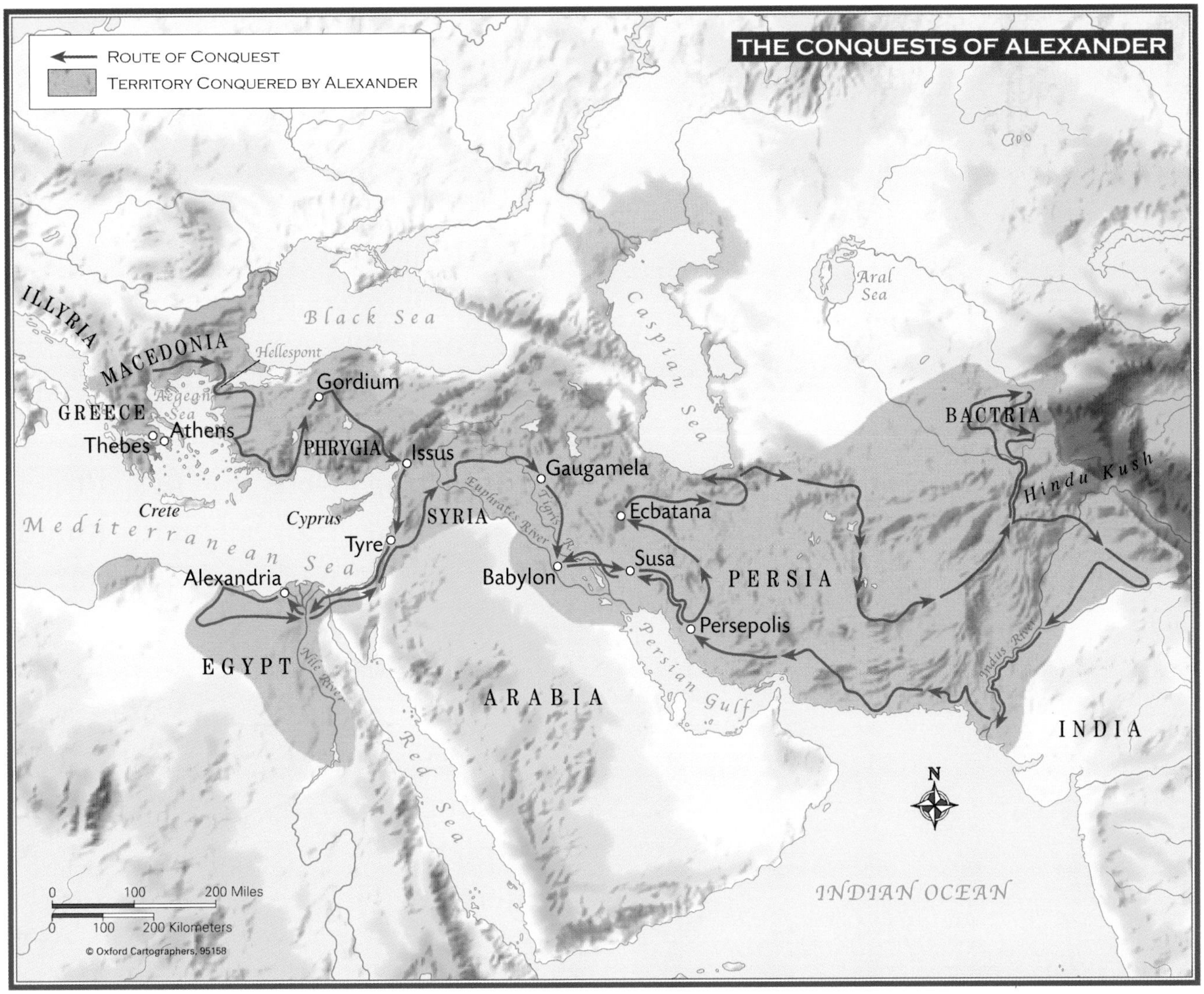

After the Battle of Issus, Alexander led his army into Egypt and Mesopotamia. He claimed to be freeing these lands from the Persians, who had conquered them several centuries earlier. In reality he was simply claiming them for himself. He continued into Persia, the heartland of the enemy empire, and then on into the regions beyond Persia's eastern borders. Within a few years, he ruled an empire far larger than the Persian empire at its height.

Mountains and crossed the Indus River into India. There Alexander met well-trained soldiers who rode armored elephants, and still his troops were victorious. However, they were also tired and **mutinous**. In 326 they refused to continue eastward, so Alexander headed back toward Persia. He spent several months setting his Persian kingdom in order before preparing to invade Arabia, another prize he wished to add to his empire. Before he could do so, though, Alexander the Great fell sick and died in Babylon at the age of thirty-two.

The Hellenistic Age

Alexander the Great had hoped to create a single, united empire across the known world. His death ended that dream,

Writers during Alexander's lifetime and soon afterward described him as handsome and strong. He is usually shown as a heroic figure—good looking, youthful, and powerful in war—as in this image, created in Italy several centuries after his death.

because he had not named a king to rule after him. The realm that he had fought so hard to assemble fell apart as his generals and followers argued over control of pieces of the once-mighty empire. Alexander's vast lands were carved into smaller kingdoms. The largest and longest-lasting were Egypt's Ptolemaic kingdom and the Seleucid kingdom, which covered Asia Minor and part of the old Persian empire.

Alexander had planned to hellenize his empire, or spread Greek culture, language, ideas, and architecture throughout it. Although his death left this process incomplete, it also left the eastern Mediterranean and much of western Asia dotted with Greek-style forts, towns, and cities. Many of these settlements were occupied by Greek soldiers who had married local women. Temples to Greek gods rose in regions as far away as Bactria. Along the frontiers of Alexander's conquests, local languages absorbed many Greek names and words. Closer to home, Greek language, art, and systems of learning dominated the eastern Mediterranean. Because of this widespread influence, the several centuries after Alexander's death are known as the Hellenistic Age.

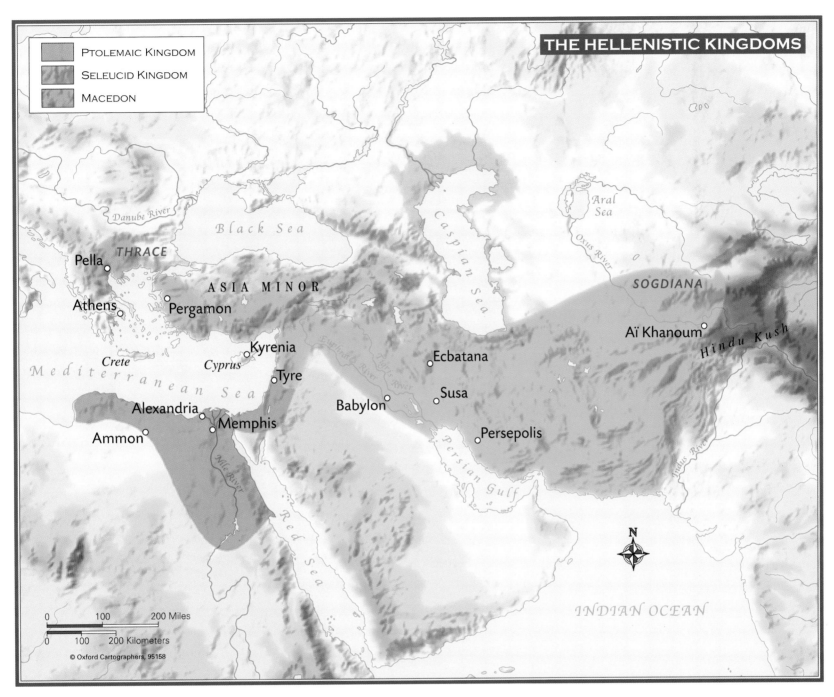

THE HELLENISTIC KINGDOMS

Legend:
- Ptolemaic Kingdom
- Seleucid Kingdom
- Macedon

Danube River · Black Sea · THRACE · Pella · Athens · ASIA MINOR · Pergamon · Crete · Cyprus · Kyrenia · Tyre · Mediterranean Sea · Alexandria · Memphis · Ammon · Nile River · Red Sea · Babylon · Euphrates River · Tigris River · Ecbatana · Susa · Persepolis · Persian Gulf · Caspian Sea · Aral Sea · Oxus River · SOGDIANA · Aï Khanoum · Hindu Kush · Indus River · INDIAN OCEAN

0 100 200 Miles
0 100 200 Kilometers
© Oxford Cartographers, 95158

After Alexander's death, Macedonia remained a small independent kingdom, but its power was all but gone. It never again played much of a role in affairs beyond its borders. But two parts of Alexander's empire turned into large, powerful kingdoms. Ptolemy, Alexander's chief spy, seized control of Egypt. He and his descendants—called the Ptolemaic dynasty—ruled Egypt for three centuries. Seleucus, one of Alexander's generals, took control of Persia, Mesopotamia, and Asia Minor. This vast region became the Seleucid kingdom. Together the Ptolemaic and Seleucid realms were the chief powers in the Hellenistic, or Greek-influenced, world.

Mapping the Heavens and the Earth

Alexandria, Egypt, was a center of learning in the Hellenistic Age, with its many schools and huge library. One important Alexandrian scholar was Claudius Ptolemaeus, known as Ptolemy, who lived and worked in the city in the 100s C.E. He wrote the *Almagest,* a book on astronomy that summarized ancient scientists' ideas about the heavens and included Ptolemy's own careful observations of stars and planets. It shaped astronomical thinking for almost 1,500 years. Even more influential was Ptolemy's *Geography,* which described principles and methods for mapmakers to follow. No maps made by Ptolemy survive, but the *Geography* was reprinted often between the 1100s and the 1600s C.E. Arabic and European mapmakers drew many maps using Ptolemy's information and methods. These are called Ptolemaic maps. Many of Ptolemy's mapmaking tools are still used today. For example, Ptolemy invented the grid system known as lines of latitude and longitude that lets mapmakers pinpoint any spot on Earth's surface.

One of the most learned citizens of Hellenistic Egypt was Claudius Ptolemaeus, or Ptolemy, who wrote books on astronomy and geography. His ideas influenced European thinkers for centuries. In the 1660s C.E. Dutch mapmaker Joannes Janssonius made this chart of the heavens based on Ptolemy's astronomical work.

Alexander the Great had united the eastern Mediterranean and western Asia under the rule of one man. The next great power in those regions was not a single conqueror, but a nation that grew ever more mighty and aggressive. From its capital city on the Italian peninsula, Rome extended its influence and control over most of the ancient Mediterranean world.

By 280 B.C.E. almost all of the peninsula had come under Roman rule. Only a few Greek cities in southern Italy remained independent. In 272 B.C.E. the largest of these cities, Tarentum, fell to the Romans, sending shock waves through the Hellenistic world. One Greek leader called Rome "the cloud rising in the west."

Because of the rivalries and alliances that had existed in Greece after Alexander's death, city-states formed regional groups such as the Aetolian and Achaean Leagues. In the 200s B.C.E. the Macedonians again tried to rule Greece, but their attempt failed and Greece was never united. The much-feared Roman invasion began in 197 B.C.E. when Rome drove the Macedonian armies out of Greece and later made Macedonia a Roman territory. The Romans, admirers of Greek culture, claimed that they had freed Greece.

The "freed" Greeks feared that Rome would conquer them next. They were right. Rome defeated the Achaean League in battle and burned the city of Corinth to the ground to show what would happen to any city-state that resisted Roman rule. By 146 B.C.E. Rome had taken possession of Greece and reorganized its governments. Although the Romans gave Athens and Sparta a degree of independence, no one doubted that Rome was the new master of the Mediterranean.

CHAPTER THREE
Rome

Much of what we know about the Etruscans comes from the colorful, lifelike images they made to decorate their tombs. Many such tombs still exist north of Rome. The tomb paintings show the Etruscans dining, hunting, and enjoying music and sports.

Rome was the largest ancient Mediterranean power—and the last. From a handful of farming villages along Italy's Tiber River, it became an empire spanning much of Europe, North Africa, and western Asia. Its fall, after a thousand years, marked the end of the ancient world. But Rome's influence was long lasting. The states that arose in Europe after the empire's decline inherited the laws, language, culture, and architecture of ancient Rome.

THE KINGDOM

The first Romans lived in settlements perched on a cluster of hilltops on the southern bank of the Tiber around 1000 B.C.E. Over time these villages grew larger and began trading with other communities. To the north lived the Etruscans, whose culture was influenced by the Greeks. The Romans adopted many elements of Etruscan culture, including an alphabet, religious beliefs, artistic styles, and the idea of the city-state. By 600 B.C.E. Rome had become a city-state that controlled the Tiber Valley.

Rome was also a monarchy, ruled by a king. Roman historians writing hundreds of years later claimed that Rome had seven kings beginning in 753 B.C.E. Archaeologists doubt that this account is completely true, but they do know that Roman kings did rule in the 600s and 500s B.C.E. The kings were religious as well as political leaders, responsible for influencing the gods in Rome's favor. Roman kings ruled for life, but unlike most ancient monarchs they were chosen by the city's leading families. That system

An Etruscan sarcophagus, a container made to hold either a body or a smaller coffin containing a body. This sarcophagus dates from the sixth century B.C.E. and was designed for a husband and wife.

reflects an idea that would be central to Roman rule: even the most powerful government depends on the consent and choice of the people.

Some of Rome's later kings were Etruscans. Under their rule Romans developed a taste for Greek art and poetry and began building shrines and temples like those of the Greeks. By 510 B.C.E., however, the Romans felt that their king, Tarquin, had become an unjust tyrant. They rebelled, threw him out of Rome, and created a new form of government.

THE REPUBLIC

Rome's new government was a republic, a state run by officials the citizens elected. The top officials were two consuls elected to one-year terms. Citizen assemblies had various powers and could limit the consuls' actions.

At first Rome's **patricians**, its wealthy and noble classes, generally controlled the assemblies because their votes counted for more than those of the **plebeians**, or common citizens. Over the centuries, though, the plebeians won more political

A female wolf nurtures the twins Romulus and Remus, characters from one of Rome's oldest myths. The wolf became a symbol of Roman strength and pride.

Rome's Legendary Origins

The Romans had several legends about their city's origins. One tale dating from the 300s B.C.E. told of Romulus and Remus, twin boys thrown into the Tiber River as babies but rescued by a female wolf and a woodpecker. The twins built the city on the spot where they had come to rest on the river's bank. Later Romulus killed his brother and became the first king of the city called Rome in his honor. The second legend formed the basis of the *Aeneid*, an epic poem written between 30 and 19 B.C.E. by the poet Virgil. His mythological account of the origins and destiny of Rome claims that the city's founder was Aeneas, a heroic prince of ancient times who survived the Trojan War. According to Virgil, the gods told Aeneas to build on the banks of the Tiber a great city that would one day rule the world. Romans loved this legend for two reasons. It claimed that they were descended from an ancient prince, making them as long-established and noble as the Greeks. And by saying that the gods wanted Rome to rule the world, the *Aeneid* seemed to give divine support for Rome's many wars of conquest and expansion.

rights. They began holding consulships and other high offices, and by 287 B.C.E. they had become Rome's chief lawmakers. Rome was still strongly divided by class, but the divisions now involved money as much as noble birth. Wealthy Romans—whether patrician or plebeian—bought votes and key positions and thus controlled Roman politics.

The Roman republic grew by conquering its neighbors on the Italian peninsula, including the Etruscans. Its first serious setback came in 387 B.C.E., when a northern tribe called the Gauls attacked and looted the city of Rome. Eventually the Romans drove the invaders back to northern Italy and returned to the business of conquest. By 272 Rome had captured Tarentum and other Greek cities in southern Italy. These conquests brought the Romans into contact—and conflict—with other strong Mediterranean powers. But Rome rose to the challenge, built a navy, and continued to expand.

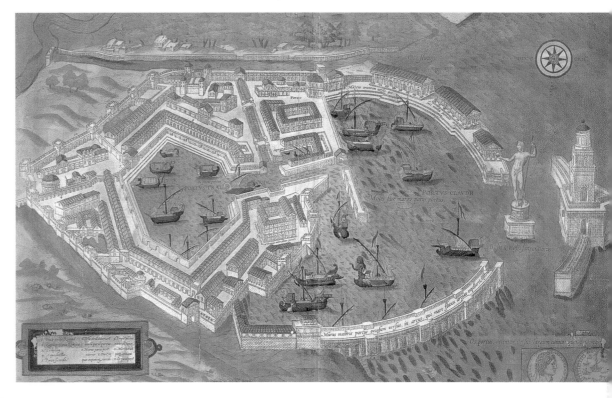

Legend says that the Romans founded a settlement at Ostia, near the mouth of the Tiber River, to get salt from the shallow sea pools there. Later Ostia became a key Roman port. It was the headquarters of the Roman fleet on the west coast of Italy, and it was where shipments of foreign grain—essential to Rome's survival—entered the capital. In the late sixteenth century C.E., mapmakers Georg Braun and Frans Hogenberg created an image of Ostia as it may have looked in the days of the empire.

CONQUEST AND WAR

Carthage was a North African city-state that had been settled by Phoenicians, people from the eastern Mediterranean. The seafaring Carthaginians had built a western Mediterranean trade empire that included the islands of Sicily, Sardinia, and Corsica off Italy's western coast. These islands, however,

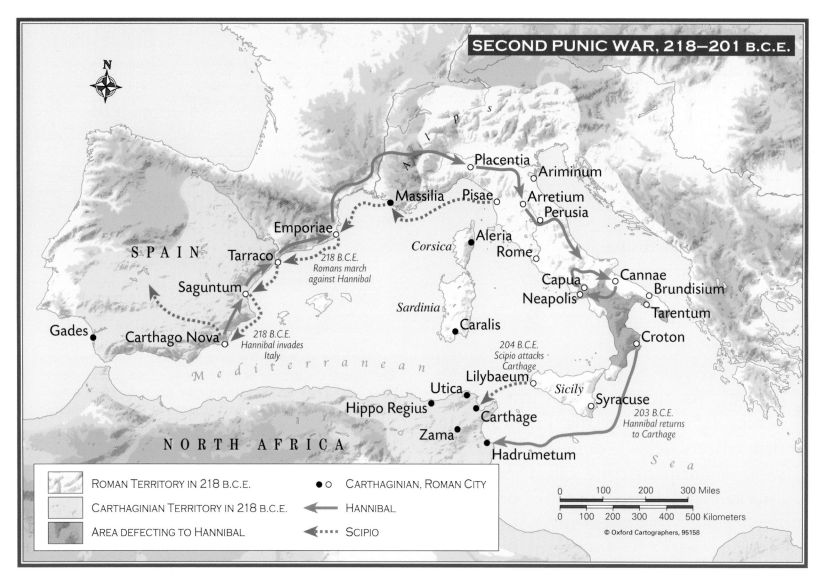

SECOND PUNIC WAR, 218–201 B.C.E.

N

SPAIN

Gades

Carthago Nova

Saguntum

Tarraco

Emporiae

218 B.C.E.
Romans march
against Hannibal

218 B.C.E.
Hannibal invades
Italy

Massilia

Pisae

Placentia

Ariminum

Arretium
Perusia

Rome

Corsica

Aleria

Sardinia

Caralis

M e d i t e r r a n e a n

Capua
Neapolis

Cannae
Brundisium

Tarentum

Croton

Lilybaeum

Sicily

Syracuse

203 B.C.E.
Hannibal returns
to Carthage

204 B.C.E.
Scipio attacks
Carthage

Utica

Hippo Regius

Zama

Carthage

Hadrumetum

NORTH AFRICA

S e a

ROMAN TERRITORY IN 218 B.C.E.

CARTHAGINIAN TERRITORY IN 218 B.C.E.

AREA DEFECTING TO HANNIBAL

● ○ CARTHAGINIAN, ROMAN CITY

HANNIBAL

SCIPIO

0   100   200   300 Miles

0 100 200 300 400 500 Kilometers

© Oxford Cartographers, 95158

In the Second Punic War, Rome faced a bold and determined enemy: Hannibal, a general from Carthage on the North African coast. In 218 B.C.E. Hannibal led his army—including trained elephants—along the coast of Spain and France. The Romans, led by a general named Scipio, attacked Hannibal's army at several points along the route but could not stop its advance. The Carthaginians never attacked Rome, but they did march deep into southern Italy. Later, in 205, Scipio sailed from Sicily to attack Carthage, prompting Hannibal to leave Italy and return to defend his homeland. Scipio then defeated him and forced him into exile. The Second Punic War left Rome the main power in the Mediterranean world.

"This was the noblest Roman of them all," wrote William Shakespeare in his play *Julius Caesar*. Caesar was extremely popular with the people of Rome, but the senators feared him because they suspected he wanted to make himself king and limit their power. Their fear and suspicion led them to murder him in 44 B.C.E.

were important places that Rome would need to control if it were to dominate more than just the Italian peninsula.

Rome and Carthage fought three wars, called the Punic Wars, between 264 and 146 B.C.E. In the first war, Rome captured Sicily. In the second, a Carthaginian general named Hannibal led an army from Spain across the Alps and into Italy. The Romans eventually forced Hannibal to surrender, gaining control of Spain and some North African territory in the process. In the third Punic War, Rome destroyed Carthage. By that time Rome had also driven the Gauls out of northern Italy, conquered Macedonia and Greece, and begun its conquest of Asia Minor.

The Roman republic prospered from rapid expansion, but its success in conquering foreign territory led to trouble on the home front. Rich Romans grew richer—but the poor became poorer and more rebellious. A series of uprisings and civil wars gripped the city as mobs, political groups, generals, and consuls struggled for power. In 60 B.C.E. two consuls and a general named Julius Caesar joined forces to control the government. Caesar went on to conquer Gaul (now called France) and emerged as a popular hero to his soldiers. As for the consuls, one died in Asia Minor and the other turned against the general. Civil war raged until Caesar declared himself dictator. One of his goals was to ease tensions between the rich and poor. Before he could do so, however, he was assassinated in 44 B.C.E. by senators who feared that he would restore the monarchy and drain the senate, Rome's highest assembly, of its power.

Caesar's death sparked a new civil war within the Roman republic, whose government had been unraveling for years. After more than a decade of power struggles, battles, and betrayals among a handful of patricians and generals, Caesar's nephew Octavian,

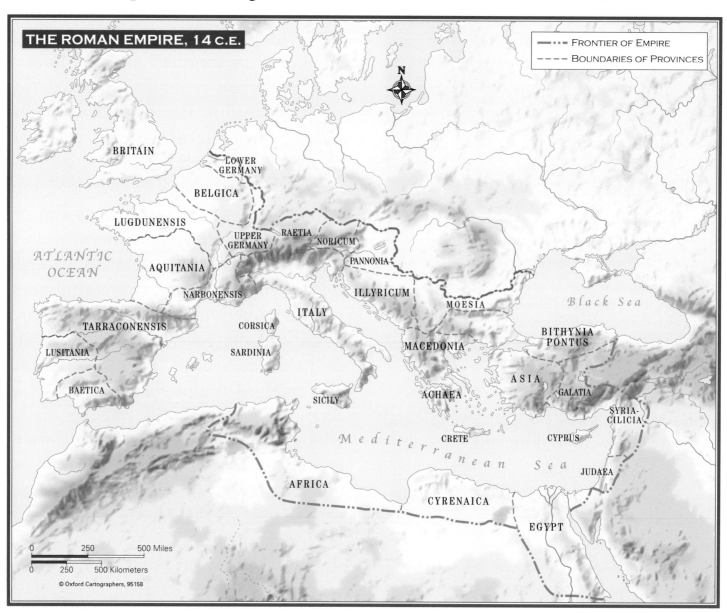

THE ROMAN EMPIRE, 14 C.E.

—·—·— FRONTIER OF EMPIRE
— — — BOUNDARIES OF PROVINCES

N

BRITAIN

LOWER GERMANY

BELGICA

LUGDUNENSIS

UPPER GERMANY

RAETIA

NORICUM

PANNONIA

ATLANTIC OCEAN

AQUITANIA

NARBONENSIS

ILLYRICUM

MOESIA

Black Sea

ITALY

TARRACONENSIS

CORSICA

MACEDONIA

BITHYNIA PONTUS

LUSITANIA

SARDINIA

ASIA

GALATIA

BAETICA

SICILY

ACHAEA

SYRIA-CILICIA

CRETE

CYPRUS

Mediterranean Sea

JUDAEA

AFRICA

CYRENAICA

EGYPT

0   250   500 Miles
0   250   500 Kilometers

© Oxford Cartographers, 95158

Through conquests and treaties, Augustus Caesar, the first Roman emperor, acquired a huge amount of foreign territory for Rome. When he died in 14 C.E. he left a well-organized empire divided into many provinces. Augustus encouraged thousands of Italian peasants to immigrate to the provinces by offering them free land. This accomplished two goals. It helped relieve overcrowding, poverty, and unrest in Italy, and it created a population loyal to Augustus in the provinces. In later years, though, few Italians were interested in moving to the remote reaches of the empire. Instead, foreigners from the provinces migrated to Rome, making the city a cultural and ethnic melting pot.

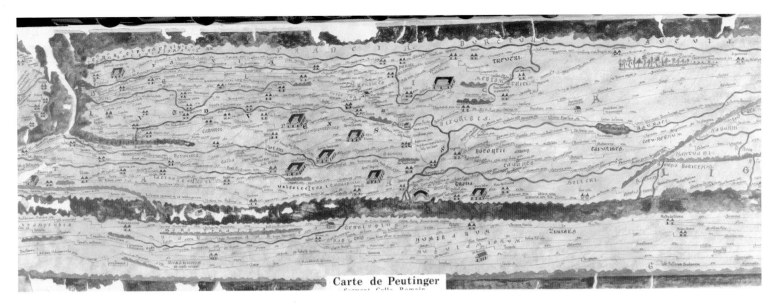

Carte de Peutinger

Roman mapmakers did not concern themselves with the shape of the world or the geography of distant lands. Their job was to help armies and goods efficiently travel the roads of the empire. The original version of this ancient Roman road map has been lost for centuries, but a copy made sometime around 1200 C.E. shows the Romans' practical approach to mapmaking. Details on the map tell of road conditions, distances between water sources, and places to sleep.

later called Augustus, took control of the senate in 27 B.C.E. Claiming that he would safeguard the principles of the republic, Augustus drew all the reins of control into his own hands. His supporters rallied the senate to give him more and more powers until it was clear that the republic was dead. Augustus had become Rome's first emperor.

Augustus ruled until his death in 14 C.E. His reign was a time of prosperity, growth, and stable government for Rome. The years that followed were less so. Emperors came to the throne not just by inheriting the title from their uncles or fathers, but sometimes by simply seizing power. The position grew dangerous. Many emperors died from acts of violence rather than natural causes. Nero, for example, killed himself in 68 C.E. during a revolt; Domitian was murdered in 96 C.E. by a group that included his wife and bodyguards; and Commodus was strangled in 192 C.E. while wrestling. Throughout these years the army shaped the empire's fate, often using the threat of violence to place favorite generals on the throne.

The years between 235 and 284 C.E. brought Rome to an especially low point. More than twenty emperors ruled, most of them badly. Eastern territories rebelled. Barbarians, as the Romans called the peoples living outside the empire, attacked the northern frontier. Fortunately for Rome, a capable emperor named Diocletian came to the throne in 284 C.E. and strengthened the empire's borders.

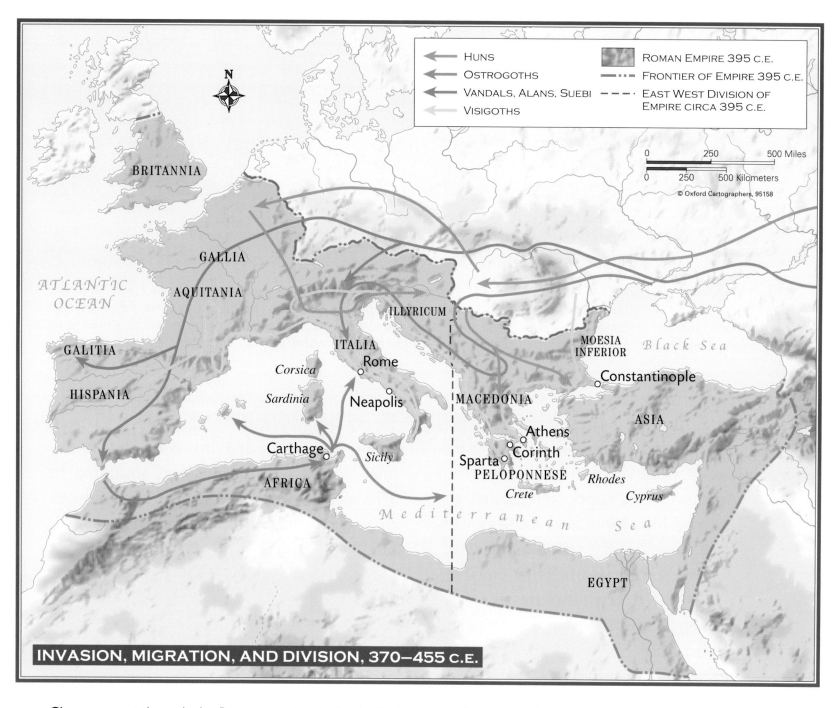

INVASION, MIGRATION, AND DIVISION, 370–455 C.E.

Legend:

- **Huns**
- **Ostrogoths**
- **Vandals, Alans, Suebi**
- **Visigoths**
- **Roman Empire 395 C.E.**
- **Frontier of Empire 395 C.E.**
- **East West Division of Empire circa 395 C.E.**

© Oxford Cartographers, 95158

Change swept through the Roman empire during its final century. The empire had been divided into eastern and western sections. Many of the wealthiest provinces were in the eastern empire. Without the income from their taxes, the western empire fell into economic decline. At the same time, waves of powerful foreign warriors attacked from the east and north, and most of their attacks were aimed at the western empire. As the split between the two empires widened, the eastern portion created its own version of Christianity so that it would be independent of the church authorities in Rome. When the western empire finally collapsed and barbarians overran Rome, the eastern empire concentrated on protecting its own borders.

After Diocletian, two leaders won control of different parts of the empire: Licinius in the east and Constantine in Rome. Then in 324 C.E. Constantine defeated Licinius and took control of the entire empire. His reign brought two major changes. First, Constantine became a Christian and made Christianity—which many earlier emperors had outlawed—a lawful religion. From that time the number of Roman converts to Christianity grew, as did the power of the Christian church. Second, Constantine moved the capital of the empire east to the ancient Greek city of Byzantium, which he renamed Constantinople. From that time on, the western half of the empire, centered in Rome, began to lose power.

One of Constantine's heirs, the emperor Julian, tried to turn back time by restoring the ancient Greek and Roman religions and limiting the power of the Christians. Julian showed great promise as a ruler, but he died during a military campaign in Persia before having the chance to make many changes. The Roman empire continued to grow increasingly unorganized and hard to govern, and in 395 C.E. it was formally divided into a western empire and an eastern empire.

The western empire endured repeated attacks by barbarian armies from Gaul, Germany, and eastern Europe. In 410 a people called the Visigoths invaded Italy from the north, looting Rome as the Gauls had done eight hundred years earlier. The imperial capital had been moved to the city of Ravenna, but the attack on Rome opened the way for the Visigoths to seize more Roman territory. Soon another group, the Vandals, invaded Roman North Africa and used it as a base for attacks on the Italian mainland. In 451 Rome briefly joined forces with several barbarian kingdoms to defeat a new enemy, the Huns of eastern Europe, led by the warlord Attila. But this shaky alliance did not last. In 476 C.E. a barbarian king named Odoacer drove Romulus Augustulus, the last Roman emperor, from the throne. The western Roman empire had finally collapsed.

The eastern portion, which became known as the Byzantine empire, survived attacks by both Huns and Persians. In 527 C.E. its emperor, Justinian I, tried but

The End of the Ancient World?

The Roman historian Procopius recorded a spell of strange weather in 535 and 536 C.E., when "the sun gave forth its light without brightness like the moon during this whole year." A Greek of the same time wrote of the "Dark Sun." One Italian official, worried about the food supply, wrote, "The months which should have been maturing the crops have been chilled by north winds."

The eerie weather reached far beyond the Mediterranean. The 1999 book called *Catastrophe*, by journalist and archaeological expert David Keys, contains accounts of darkness, cold, severe storms, droughts, and crop failures around the world in 535 and 536. Keys suspects that a major event, probably a volcanic eruption in Southeast Asia, caused the strange weather. The eruption shot dust and gas into the air, where it remained for years, altering the world's climate. According to Keys, the climate changes may have had far-reaching effects, producing plagues and famines that toppled some ancient civilizations, including the Mexican city-state of Teotihuacán. The climate changes also led to mass migrations of peoples such as the Avars, who left their homeland in Mongolia and eventually settled in eastern Europe, where they fought the Byzantine empire. Keys argues that the natural disaster "altered world history dramatically and permanently" by causing events that brought a close to the ancient period and let new nations and cultures emerge. If Keys is right, could another natural disaster beyond human control again change the course of world history?

Justinian I, ruler of the eastern or Byzantine empire, briefly gained control of some former Roman territory in Italy and North Africa. His attempt to reunite the old empire died with him, though, but one of his reforms had lasting results. To promote Christianity, Justinian ordered the closing of the schools that taught other philosophies and religions. Some historians see Justinian's reign, not the fall of Rome, as the true end of the ancient Mediterranean world.

failed to recapture some of the western empire. Two years later, Justinian shut down all the pagan, or non-Christian, schools located throughout the Byzantine empire. The closing of these schools cut one of the last ties with the ancient Greek and Hellenistic past. The Byzantine empire remained in existence as a Christian power in the eastern Mediterranean for a thousand years, throughout the Middle Ages.

Glossary

alliance—An agreement to help one another or work together to reach a shared goal.

archaeologist—One who studies the physical traces of past cultures and civilizations.

artifact—An object made by humans.

Asia Minor—The peninsula across the Aegean Sea from Greece, today known as the nation of Turkey.

colony—A territory controlled by a country but outside that country's borders.

fertility—Fruitfulness; the ability to bring forth new plant, animal, or human life.

migration—The movement of individuals or whole peoples from one region to another.

mutinous—Resisting orders and refusing to recognize a leader's authority.

myths—A body of legends and stories based on tradition and religion rather than history.

patrician—A member of Rome's upper class.

plague—A severe and widespread outbreak of deadly disease.

plebeian—A member of Rome's lower class; a commoner.

prehistory—The period before writing existed.

republic—A form of government headed by elected representatives and lawmakers.

2200–1400 B.C.E. Minoan civilization flourishes on Crete.

1400–1200 B.C.E. Mycenaean civilization reaches its height in Greece.

776 The Greeks hold the first Olympic Games.

753 According to legend, Rome is founded.

750–500 The Greeks establish colonies around the Mediterranean Sea.

509 The kingdom of Rome ends, and the Roman republic begins.

499–479 Greeks fight the Persian Wars.

460–429 Pericles governs Athens.

431–404 Greek city-states fight one another in the Peloponnesian Wars.

334–323 Alexander the Great builds a Greek empire in Asia.
.

323 The Hellenistic period begins.

264–146 Rome fights Carthage in three conflicts called the Punic Wars.

146 Greece comes under Roman rule.

49–45 Civil war flares up in Rome.

31 The Roman republic ends, and the Roman empire begins.

43 C.E. Britain becomes a province of the Roman empire.

200s German tribes start raiding the Roman empire.

313 The emperor Constantine gives Christianity legal protection.

395 The Roman empire is divided into a western empire, based in Rome, and an eastern empire, based in Constantinople.

410 A German tribe called the Visigoths sacks Rome.

450s Huns battle their way to power in Europe.

476 The western Roman empire ends. The eastern empire continues under the rule of Christian emperors.

529 The eastern Roman emperor Justinian closes non-Christian schools.

Chronology

Further Reading

BOOKS

Ash, Maureen. *Alexander the Great.* Chicago: Children's Press, 1991.

Baker, Rosalie. *Ancient Romans.* New York: Oxford University Press, 1998.

Burrell, Roy. *First Ancient History.* New York: Oxford University Press, 1994.

Corbishley, Mike. *Ancient Rome: Cultural Atlas for Young People.* New York: Facts on File, 2003.

———. *Everyday Life in Roman Times.* New York: Franklin Watts, 1994.

Daly, Kathleen. *Greek and Roman Mythology A to Z: A Young Reader's Companion.* New York: Facts on File, 1992.

Greece: Temples, Tombs & Treasures. Alexandria, VA: Time-Life Books, 1994.

James, Simon. *Ancient Rome.* New York: Dorling Kindersley, 2000.

Macdonald, Fiona. *How Would You Survive as an Ancient Greek?* New York: Franklin Watts, 1995.

Nardo, Don. *Ancient Greece.* San Diego: Lucent Books, 1994.

———. *The Roman Empire.* San Diego: Lucent Books, 1994.

———. *The Roman Republic.* San Diego: Lucent Books, 1994.

Sheehan, Sean. *Illustrated Encyclopedia of Ancient Greece.* Los Angeles: J. Paul Getty Museum, 2002.

Stefoff, Rebecca. *The Palace of Minos at Knossos.* New York: Oxford University Press, 2003.

———. *Rome: Echoes of Imperial Glory.* Alexandria, VA: Time-Life Books, 1994.

Whittock, Martyn. *The Roman Empire.* New York: Peter Bedrick Books, 1996.

WEB SITES

www.carlos.emory.edu/ODYSSEY/NEAR EAST/homepg.html
The Near East—Cradle of Civilization, maintained by Emory University's Michael C. Carlos Museum, has sections on Greece and Rome that explore archaeology, people, mythology, daily life, death and burial, and other topics.

www.dalton.org/groups/rome
Maintained by New York's Dalton School, this site includes sections on Roman politics, literature, and other topics.

www.wings.buffalo.edu/Maecenas/general_contents/
This site contains more than 2,000 color and black-and-white photographs of archaeological relics of classical Greece and Rome.

www.ce.eng.usf.edu/pharos/wonders/
This site is devoted to the Seven Wonders of the Ancient World, some of which were Greek and Hellenistic.

www.members.aol.com/Donnclass/Romelife/
Daily Life in Ancient Rome is an entertaining site with descriptions of typical Roman clothes, meals, holidays, and families.

ABOUT THE AUTHOR

Rebecca Stefoff is the author of Marshall Cavendish's North American Historical Atlases series, the *Young Oxford Companion to Maps and Mapmaking*, and many other nonfiction books for children and young adults, including books on the ancient civilizations of the Near East and the Minoan culture of Crete. History, geography, and maps are among her special interests. In recent years Stefoff has enjoyed traveling to many ancient Greek and Roman sites in the Mediterranean world. She makes her home in Portland, Oregon. You can find a list of her books at www.rebeccastefoff.com.

Index

Page numbers in **boldface** are illustrations.